A Boy From Haggerston

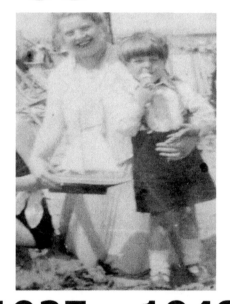

1927 – 1948
by
Ben Flude

Published in 2024 by FeedARead.com Publishing

A CIP catalogue record for this title is available from the British Library.

The Book was edited by Kevin Flude

Cover Photograph shows the Author with his mother at Hastings c1930.

HAGGERSTON
(1927 - 1931)

Emily Ada Prosser - Aged 16

It all began in Haggerston on the 1st of October 1927, when I was born at 1.00 a.m., in my parents' room on the top floor of 16 Lee Street. My Mum was called Emily Ada Flude (née Prosser), but she was known to everyone as Emmy. My Dad, Arthur Benjamin Flude was known as Ben. To avoid confusion, I was to be known as Benny.

Where is Haggerston, you may well ask? It is in East London between Shoreditch and Dalston. It had been a small village surrounded by open fields in the late 17th Century. But as building on a large scale started in the mid-18th century, and accelerated with the coming of the Regent's Canal and the Railway, Haggerston quickly became a busy, working-class area.

At the time I was born, it was in the Metropolitan Borough of Shoreditch, which later merged with Hackney and Stoke Newington in 1965 to form the London Borough of Hackney. It has always been a working-class area, although now it is somewhat trendy and, as some say, overflowing with Hackney Hipsters. And, like most of London, today it is a crowded, busy jungle.

Mum and Dad lived in rooms upstairs in 16, Lee Street, which is near to Haggerston Overground Station. They shared the toilet with Mrs Lea, the lady who lived downstairs. As far as I know, there was no bathroom.

My Mum left school at 14 years old, and went to work as a cook in the staff canteen at Bovril's factory and offices in Old Street. The factory was opposite to Henry Street, where she lived then. Everyone said my Mum was a great cook. My children used to love going to her house on a Saturday, as she made a superb tea of egg, bacon, beans and chips. Kevin, my son, tells me he has never tasted better fried eggs, and he hated going to her house on a Sunday as that was the day for cucumber sandwiches rather than the fry-up he loved.

The Bovril factory was set up in 1889 to produce a meat extract from beef. Scott, Shackleton and Edmund Hilary's expeditions were powered by tea made from Bovril. The beef was from Argentina. In 1924, the company introduced 'Marmite' and in 1935, Ambrosia Creamed Rice. All three can still be purchased.

At the Bovril factory, my mum met and became great friends with Ethel Flude, and it was through her that she met my Dad, Ben, Ethel's brother. I remember that Ethel and Mum used to love going 'up West' for an evening's entertainment in the West End.

My mum must have met Dad at some point in 1922 before they got married in 1924. She told me that when he called for her, her younger sister, Nelly, used to hide under the table because she feared uniforms. This suggests he was still in the RAF and not yet demobbed. When they got married, he was employed as a 'rigger' or an aircraft mechanic with the Imperial Airways at Croydon Airport.

My Dad's family were a family of Benjamins. His Dad, my Grandad, Benjamin, was a walking stick maker but had previously been, in his youth, an umbrella maker. In fact, all of Grandad Flude's family had been involved in making umbrellas - each member making a different part. Frederick Flude, my Great Grandad, lived in Dalston and was also in the umbrella trade. In those days,

Arthur Benjamin Flude. RAF c1918

umbrellas were called Gamps. You may have heard of Dickens' character, Mrs Sairey Gamp, from Martin

um (in her dyed wedding dress) and Dad with Lizzie, Edith, Charles and two of my cousins

Chuzzlewit, who always carried an umbrella with "particular ostentation" and so gave her name to the brolly.

My Dad had one brother (Charles Francis Flude) and four sisters. Lizzie was the eldest. Then, came Edith, Dad, Ethel and May. May was the youngest and later married Fred Jacobs. Fred's father used to keep his wife short of money, and she had to resort to taking money out of his pockets when he returned drunk from the pub.

My parents married on Christmas Day 1924. He was 24 and she was 22. As soon as they married, Mum had to leave her job, which was how things were done in those days. Sadly, they only enjoyed married life for four years.

In July 1928, before I' d reached my first birthday, my Dad died in Croydon Hospital. He had previously been taken sick at work and had to have an operation for a perforated duodenal ulcer. Although he had recovered and returned to work, it perforated again in July, and he died. If this were to happen today, it could be easily cured, but in those days it was a death sentence.

The ulcer was an inherited condition from his father, which was also passed on to me. I have had two perforated duodenal ulcers and one gastric ulcer throughout my life. All three were cured by medical treatment and not viewed as serious given the advances in medical science. My son, Kevin, and my granddaughter, Hetty, have also had some stomach or reflux problems, possibly stemming from the same susceptibility.

It has always been a great sadness to me that I never knew my father. I was 9 months old when he died, and he was just 28 years old. Everyone seemed to like him, and as a child, he was always my hero. In my imagination, I promoted him to being a brilliant and brave Ace RAF Pilot. But he was, in fact, a mechanic rather than a pilot in World War I. Following the war, he worked with Imperial Airways in Purley, Croydon. I don't know the exact details and so have to piece the story together from the little information I have at my disposal.

My friend, Roy, tells me that the badge on his uniform in the oval picture is of the Royal Flying Corp. (RFC). But they were disbanded in 1916/17, and replaced by the RAF thereafter. As my dad was born in 1900, he must have joined up to fight in the war while underage at 16 or 17 as a volunteer. Beddington Aerodrome, in Purley, was an RFC base to combat Zeppelin Raids, flying B.E 2C's in 1916. This base subsequently transferred to the RAF, and after the war merged with Wadden Aerodrome to form the civilian Croydon Airport.

The two aerodromes were on either side of Plough Lane, in Purley, and traffic had to be controlled by a set of traffic lights when aeroplanes were landing! Although this may sound primitive, in 1920 the Airport was the world's first to introduce air traffic control, and had the world's first Control Tower and first airport terminal.

Dad is standing tall in the back row extreme right

I know that Dad worked for Imperial Airways as an Aircraft mechanic. The airline was formed in 1924, and later merged into BOAC and later British Airways. At some point, Dad must have left the RAF and become a civilian aircraft mechanic. How he got into the industry in the first place, we don't know, but the family background in making umbrellas would have given him a knowledge of working with wood, metal and fabric - which is what early planes were made of. His job was a 'Rigger'. I have no idea how he got to Croydon every day from Haggerston, but he could have got a tram to London Bridge from Lee Street and train to Croydon, which might have taken an hour or so. Or perhaps he stayed in digs.

After Dad's sudden death, Mum was immediately hard up with no income in sight, as the introduction of the State Benefit for Widows came much later. Faced with this situation, she did what widows of this part of London always did: she went office-cleaning in the nearby City of London. She used to go to work on a very early tram, using what was called a 'workman's ticket' - only available to those ticket holders who arrived at their destination before 8 a.m. They could use any tram or train on the return journey. The workman's ticket was a greatly reduced fare and was a third class ticket. They were still used in the 1960s. Thereafter, they were abolished.

Lee Street in 2022. The houses on the left are similar to the house I was born in but one story taller, and a little grander. I was born in no. 16, which was just under the bridge, to the left, where Stonebridge Park now is.

When she left home at 6:30 a.m. Mum left me in bed and Mrs Lea used to keep an eye on me until Mum came home about 3 hours later. Evidently, I was good, and Mum said that I would go on sleeping long after she came back home. Mum told Stephen and Kevin, my sons, that she used to prop me up on the settee, with cushions stopping me rolling off, and Mrs Lea would pop up from time to time to check I was OK.

16, Lee Street is above the first E in Lee

As I got older, this got much more difficult, until Auntie Ethel, one of Dad's younger sisters, brought news that the girl who had succeeded Mum at Bovril's was herself leaving to get married. Mum therefore went back to her old job. This changed everything for Mum, as Grannie and Grandad Prosser's lived near the Bovril factory. Mum could now catch a much later tram and take me to her parents, where I got into bed with them. I would lie in the middle and wait until Grannie got up to make breakfast. Grannie would get out of bed in the cold and light the range. She might come back into the bedroom to get the cold box, which was fixed to the wall outside the window of the bedroom. Here, they would keep cheese, milk and other things that needed to be kept cold. Milk was delivered, and the milkman would dispense it from a pail using a ladle into Grannie's enamel jug.

Grandad would get up next, and finally, I went from the cold bedroom to the warmth of the range where I would get dressed. On the large range was a sooty kettle and saucepan. I remember the saucepans were Judge Ware enamel. Patsy, my sister, still uses these saucepans.

There I would have a boiled egg for breakfast every day, which Mum would bring wrapped in tissue paper. If she had taken more than one egg, these would have been eaten by one of Mum's sisters, who still lived at home. I ate my egg with bread and dripping. I don't remember having butter. My Grandad had butter for the first time at the wedding reception for Rosie and her husband, Jack Grinter. Please note that, ninety years later, I am still an 'eggaholic'.

In 2013, my younger son, Kevin, moved from Clapton to Haggerston, giving me the option to revisit the place of my birth. Unfortunately, where No. 16 Lee Street should be, is now in a park. I believe the house was hit by a bomb during the war. Perhaps by the time I finish my life story, I will have found out what happened to Number 16.

My very earliest memory of living in Haggerston was picking up my 'Funny Wonder' Comic every Thursday morning from a barrow outside Haggerston Station and going by tram to Old Street. In early 1931, Nelly got married and moved out of 10, Henry Street. This left the large bedroom on the second floor empty and Mum decided that we would move in to live with Grannie and Grandad, and the two daughters, Rosie and Mary, who still lived there. So we said farewell to Haggerston and hello to Finsbury.

FINSBURY
(1931 – 1935)

Old Street. Henry Street was where the red brick building on the left now is. The Bovril Factory was across the Road where the scaffolding is.

No. 10, Henry Street, was a three-storey, terraced house with two rooms on each floor. There was no bathroom and only one toilet, which was in the yard at the rear of the house. This was where the washing was done and hung out using a washing line on a pulley. The flat had gaslighting, but not in every room and no running water, except a tap outside, in the yard. Grannie and Grandad had two rooms on the first floor with a range, for which the coal was kept in a cupboard. Annie, my Grandad's sister, lived on the ground floor. Her twin sons ran a coal business.

Mum was returning to the family home she had been brought up in with her two brothers and seven sisters. When I had children, she often told stories of her life in the house as a young girl. She remembered sharing a bed with three sisters at the head end, and two at the foot end of the bed. In those days, as no one had alarm

From Right to left. Me, Mum and three of her sisters. From l to r Florrie, Rosie, and Nellie

clocks, the street had a 'knocker-upper,' who had a long stick and would knock on the windows in the mornings to get people up in time to get to work. My son tells me that in Limehouse, the 'knocker-upper' used a pea-shooter to wake people up.

My mum told us about the street games she used to play as a child, including 'knock-down ginger', in which they would knock on people's doors and run away. She said that sometimes, they would tie up the door knocker, to the knocker next door, so that when one door opened, the other door knocker would knock! The kids also used to set up swings using the gas lamp-posts.

Life with such a large family could be stressful, and she used to show my family the scar on the back of her arm which she got when her mother, in a fury, threw a knife at her, and she lifted her hands to protect her face. Mum had no other tales of violence or abuse, so, it seems to have been very much a one-off incident. The pressure Grannie was under, is shown by what happened when she 'fell' pregnant. As Mum told it, on finding out about becoming pregnant, Grannie would disappear, and be found on the Canal Bridge at City Road, contemplating throwing herself into the Canal. It seems to have been a cry for help, and a sign that more children were the last thing she wanted.

On other stressful occasions, she would disappear from the house, and hide in Tilney Court, when she saw the 8 daughters and husband rush out to find her, she would quietly go back into the empty house. Yet, despite these stories, my Grannie and Grandad gave their many children a loving upbringing, and they both lived long and rewarding lives. I remember them both with much affection.

Mum, Grannie, Grandad

Now Mum was back in the old house in Henry Street, which was opposite the Bovril's Factory, she had no journey to make to work. The money Mum gave to Grannie and Grandad for the accommodation and our keep was a boon to them, for they were desperately poor. To add to their problems, Grandad was struck down with a form of multiple sclerosis which made walking difficult and the use of his hands painful. There were no unemployment or sickness benefits during this era, and he was too ill to go to work. At this time, he would only have been about 50. Every so often an old man known as 'Young Mr Cundle' would bring round tobacco money for Grandad. Grandad was a joiner originally and was previously Mr Cundle's foreman in the packing case construction business - presumably founded by Old Mr Cundle?

Mum got worried at this time about my health. I had always been 'a bit chesty', but this got worse when I had a series of bronchitis attacks. I also got a bout of impetigo. As we didn't have a GP because you had to pay for them, I was a frequent visitor to the Outpatients department at Bart's Hospital. They tried a number of different medicines; all horrible tasting and all proving ineffective. Mum told me, when I was a lot older, that she thought I would develop consumption - or TB as it became later known. This was very common at the time and there were no cures available. Happily, I survived, as Mum found a patent medicine at our Chemist's called Parmint[1]. It was pink and sweet and great to taste. But most importantly, it did the trick, as I soon got much better. I remember taking Parmint for many years.

The Eight Prosser Sisters BR Nellie, Annie, Mum (Emily) MR Mary, Rosie, Lizzie FR Flossie, Sarah

During this period, I made my first friend, Skippy. His full name was Scipio Leoni, and he was the youngest son of the owners of an Italian café just round the corner in Bath Street. We always played in the street using his home-made scooter in the recreation area,

---

1   Illustration from the Hobart Mercury 1917

near St Luke's Church, called Toffee Park. Under Skippy's leadership, we became more venturesome, going to Wesley's Chapel, Pitfield Street Baths and, several times to the Pictures, on City Road.

Our last visit to the Pictures, which boasted continuous performances, was to see "Dawn Patrol" with Errol Flynn, Basil Rathbone and David Niven. We went in about two o'clock and were fetched-out by our Mums at nine p.m. That was the end of our interest in the film industry! Skippy's Mum came to pick him up and boxed his ears. There were a lot of Italian, German and Irish immigrants in the area, and I remember my Grannie warning me about having anything to do with the 'Romans', by which she meant Catholics. Her maiden name was Jamieson, which possibly derives from Ulster, which might explain the reference to 'Romans'.

At home, whilst Mum was at work, Grandad used to play with me. I remember playing a game where we put

Me at a school performance. I'm the boy in the middle, dressed as the 'Spring Herald'

four chairs together to form a bus. He would be a passenger and I would let him onto the bus to sell him a ticket. He started to teach me to read and write, and tried to teach Grannie to do the same because she couldn't read. Grannie's school had nothing to do with education because she went to the Ragged School; where the girls were taught domestic skills, while the boys were taught vocational skills such as shoe repairs; window cleaning; wood and metal work. There was no reading and writing for either sex. Grannie first learned to sign her own name and do basic sums, but you could never cheat her. She was never interested in reading because Grandad used to read to her. And, as I became more proficient, I used to read a few words to her when I went to Bath Street Infants School[2]. She liked to hear poetry as well as the current news. I read a book called 'Annie and Kenneth' which had poems which she liked. One of her favourites was by John Masefield, who became Poet Laureate in 1930. It is the poem called 'Cargoes', and I can still remember some of the lines (not the first verse but the second verse).

'Cargoes'

Quinquireme of Nineveh from distant Ophir,
Rowing home to haven in sunny Palestine,
With a cargo of ivory,
And apes and peacocks,
Sandalwood, cedarwood, and sweet white wine.

Stately Spanish galleon coming from the Isthmus,
Dipping through the Tropics by the palm-green shores,
With a cargo of diamonds,

2　It was renamed Moorfields Primary School in 1951.

Emeralds, amethysts,
Topazes, and cinnamon, and gold moidores.

Dirty British coaster with a salt-caked smoke stack,
Butting through the Channel in the mad March days,
With a cargo of Tyne coal,
Road-rails, pig-lead,
Firewood, iron-ware, and cheap tin trays.

John Masefield[3]

I also remember Gray's Elegy, properly called. 'Elegy Written in a Country Churchyard' By Thomas Gray

Grannie took me to school for the first day and evidently, I cried for hours. Eventually, I began to enjoy it, especially when I was praised for my efforts at reading, writing and counting. But that praise should have been given to Grandad for all his help! I was soon made monitor by my teacher, which meant I took the register - after it had been called, and any other messages - to Miss Hall, the headmistress.

This reminds me of one event that has stuck in my mind since then. I had to take an envelope and hand it to Miss Hall and wait to bring the reply back. So off I went and knocked on her door, but was told by her secretary that I would have to wait because she was engaged. I dashed back to my teacher and told her that I could not give her the letter because she was getting married! I remember the look of disbelief that clouded her face and the gales of laughter that followed. She then gave me back my original letter together with a new note to take back to

---

3   As read by Joanna Lumley https://www.youtube.com/watch?v=zD5sZdTtjJE

the headmistress. This I did and after another bout of laughter, she gently explained another meaning of the word engaged!

While I lived on Henry Street, they changed its name to Steadman Street. After the war and after Grannie and Grandad had died, they demolished it and all the other little streets that surrounded it. Now, when you go down Old Street, you will see signs saying Steadman Court and a red-brick block of flats, built right where number 10 Henry Street used to be. When we moved away in 1935, I greatly missed the busy, happy life we had with Grannie and Grandad, and their nine children. With so many people often around, our lives were filled.

Mum also made sure that we kept in touch with my Dad's family. She made a particular effort with Grannie and Grandad Flude, and their two daughters: Auntie Ethel and Aunt Lizzie. They lived in Great Chart Street. It is up towards Hoxton, on the other side of what is now the Old Street Roundabout. But in those days, it was a cross-roads, not a roundabout.

When I was a lot older, I found out that when my Dad died, Auntie Lizzy offered to look after me until my Mum got back on her feet. She even offered to adopt me if things got desperate! Auntie Lizzie and Uncle Joe were childless, and although Mum turned down the offer, she took me to see them frequently, even when they had moved out to Kenton. Aunt Lizzie had a great big picture of my dad (the oval picture seen above). It had a little wooden model of a biplane tied to it, which I used to play with. Upon her death, I was given Dad's photograph as promised, but no one could find the plane.

At that time in my life, I spent a lot of time around City Road and Old Street. Coming out from the City, there was a cigarette factory which made the Kensitas brand.

Nearby, further on, was a little alley way or courtyard where Grandad Flude used to work making walking sticks.

Every boat race day I used to walk down to the junction with City Road and Moorfields to see the building,

Bovril Charabanc Outing, Mum, in the dark coat, is standing behind the driver. To the left of Mum is Ethel, Dad's sister

Dawson's Department Store, that announced the result of the Boat Race displaying a light blue or dark blue flag. As I remember it, we always supported Cambridge. There were a number of department stores in the City of London in those days. The one closest to Old Street, Dawsons; then Gamages was by Chancery

Lane; and the Houndsditch Warehouse near Bishopsgate.[4]

We didn't have holidays in those days, as there was not enough money nor time off work. But Mum went on work outings, as you can see from the photograph of the charabanc. Also, you will see the photo of Grannie and Granddad Prosser, looking unprepared for an outing to the sea, and the glamorous pictures of mum's younger sisters, with my mum and me at the front.

---

4   See East End memoir by Charles S. P. Jenkins who went to the same school as I did. http://www.eastend-memories.org/Places%20Lost/places-lost-2.html

LEYTON

(1935 -1940)

Margate, Grannie and Grandad on their golden wedding anniversary

In the early days of 1935, Mum dropped the bombshell that we were going to move to the "Country", and it was an even greater shock to hear that she was going to get married again! Her new husband's name was Ernie, or, to give him his full name: Ernest Elton David Martin Mosley. He was a couple of years older than my mum. Before mum told me about their upcoming marriage, I had seen him around for some time, but not guessed at the nature of their relationship. I remember that he gave me a torch as a present and taught me the trick of recharging the battery by putting it in the oven. He would eventually relent and buy me new batteries,

I'm on the left, Pop in the Middle, Patsy is the little one

but I have often wondered if the process of putting them in the oven was safe?Mum and Ernie were married in the St Leonard's Church in Shoreditch, and I was a page boy. I wore a shiny white blouse, black velvet short trousers, white cotton socks, and patent leather black shiny shoes with a strap. I thought I looked like a bit of a sissy, my male cousins agreed, but Mum and my Aunts thought I looked angelic. Thank goodness that all the wedding photos showing me in my outfit (and there weren't many in those days) have been lost! But, these days, I would not mind seeing how I looked. Maybe, I hope, I would have appeared more angelic than sissy.

Following the wedding, we said goodbye to 10 Steadman Street, EC1., and hello to 70, James Lane, Leyton, E10. I also had to say goodbye to Bath Street Infant School and hello to Canterbury Road Junior Mixed School. I found it difficult to call my step-father dad because my dad - who had become my idol, was dead. Instead, I called Ernie 'Pop' and he seemed happy with that.

70, James Lane, was a Victorian, semi-detached house in a nice, long lane that ran between High Road Leyton and Whipps Cross Road. The side entrance to Whipps Cross Hospital was at the end of James Lane. We lived in the first floor flat, while Auntie Becky (Pop's sister) and Uncle Ted (Thacker) lived below us in the ground floor flat. We shared the bathroom and garden. I think we had indoor toilets, but I remember beating our carpets in the garden with the bamboo 'rackets' used for the purpose before everyone had vacuum cleaners.

I had my own bedroom for the very first time, and it was great! It was at the back of the house and immediately opposite the bathroom. The kitchen was in the small bedroom at the front of the house, but lacked sufficient working surfaces. So Pop made a large folding table about five feet by two feet, which we laid over the bath in the bathroom when not in use. When the bath was in use, the table folded up against the wall.

We all had a weekly bath on a Friday night; ladies first, men last, with me in the middle. Becky and Mum did the washing on Mondays. I wonder whether that would be allowed today, especially as the toilet was feet away from the folding work surface. We ate on a small table in the kitchen.

Pop worked at Smithfield Market, where he was a warehouse cold-storage worker. He cycled to work every day (an eight-mile journey). Uncle Ted was a tram conductor (driver Eddie Watts). During the holidays, I often spent the day with them, as they normally worked together. My job was reversing the seat-backs on the top deck when we arrived at the terminals. The tram did not turn around, it simply reversed direction, and my job ensured the passengers always faced forward. No one seemed to mind me being there, and I remember one inspector, who would always give me a gobstopper, which seemed to change colour and last forever.

After a while, I found living in James Lane very lonely because there were very few visitors compared to Steadman Street. But we did keep in touch with both grandparents at the weekends, and with other relatives as and when my Mum would say. At about this time, I joined the Wolf Cubs at St Catherine's Church, Leyton. We were invited to the Church for a 'Magic Lantern Show' which was given by Captain Frank Worsley, who was the captain of the Endurance. This is what Wikipedia says about him.

'After the expedition's ship Endurance was trapped in pack ice and wrecked, he (Shackleton)and the rest of the crew sailed three lifeboats to Elephant Island, off the Antarctic Peninsula. From there, Worsley, Shackleton and four others sailed the 22.5-foot (6.9 m) lifeboat James Caird some 800 miles (1,300 km) across the stormy South Atlantic Ocean.'

It was a fantastic show from a real hero. I would go to the kids' cinema on Saturday mornings (at the ABC Cinema at Leytonstone) with my new-found friends, who were called Hubert Knifton and Ronnie Miles. Looking back on those days, I now think that the main reason I had difficulty settling in was that I was no longer the number one focus in my mum's life. I am sure now that I made things difficult for Pop, but he was never angry or hit me. I'm sure he got fed up with my antics, though he never said so. He also left Mum to sort out all liaison with the school.

I also found the change of schools difficult at first because I was no longer the bright one in class. The standards were much higher in Essex County Council than I had experienced in London. But I met my saviour when I met my form master, Mr Wiggs. He was a good teacher - an excellent teacher in fact! We had frequent spelling bees and mental arithmetic tests. I was excellent at the former and poor at the latter. My problem was that I was always quick to answer and therefore often wrong. Mr Wiggs' solution was "think before you answer and if you're not absolutely sure, don't respond, because if you do, it will probably be wrong." I found this to be very true and under his tutelage, even my maths improved.

Mum was suffering from terrible headaches (something many people within my family suffer from). Grandad thought it was caused by her long hair, so she had it cut. But the headaches continued. Eventually, these did get slowly better. My bronchial attacks got fewer, but Pop's painful ears got worse.

This ailment was no doubt aggravated by his cold-storage work, which he did without any appropriate ear defenders. Despite these health issues, I think we were all happy in the new house, although we never had any holidays, only the odd day trips.

Mum and all her sisters organised a day out at the seaside for Grannie and Grandad to celebrate their Golden Wedding. They had never even seen the sea before. We travelled to Margate in an old-fashioned Charabanc we had hired, with solid wheels and a hood, which we could pull up if it rained. We set off early one Sunday morning in bright sunshine, with everyone singing their hearts out until we reached a pub in Kent, where we went to "wet our whistles". Then we made our way on to Margate, where we made a big square in the sandy beach, inside which, all the kids built sand castles.

Grannie

Grannie surprised everyone by wearing a bathing costume, and with much assistance, she paddled in the sea for ages. I remember when she came back, everyone cheered. After a splendid day at the seaside, we returned home via another pub stop, where we had 'one for the road'.

We repeated this exercise three years later, when (I think) it was Grandad's birthday. This time, instead of a

Charabanc, we had a shiny new coach. The pub stops, and the beach, were as fun as they were before.

On another occasion, we had an outing to the Speedway, at Rye House, near Roydon. Speedway was a very popular form of motorcycle racing with a small dirt circuit which the teams raced around. The race was between local teams Rye House, and the Hackney Wick Wolves. We went by car, borrowed from a friend of the family (Ted Thacker), as he was the only person we knew to have a car. Pop also used to go Greyhound racing at Clapton.   The stadium was north of Millfields Road and marked by a road called Orient Way. Clapton Orient Football Club used to play here too. Mum didn't like the Greyhound racing much, but we occasionally went with Pop.

Early in 1938, I took the Scholarship, which later on became the 11-plus. There was no great expectation put upon me, and I had no pressure to do any special preparations, nor can I remember greatly wanting to go to a Grammar School. Naturally, I was pleased to hear that I had passed. However, I did not gain enough marks to get into mum's first choice, which was the Leyton County High School and just around the corner from our house. Instead, I was invited to attend an interview for the Chingford County High School, which was a new school due to open in September 1938. Mum came with me to the interview in Chingford. When I came out of it, they asked for mum to go in and speak with them. As soon as she came out, I could see from her face that I had passed. I was not aware at the time, but there were school fees to be paid, expensive blazer, cap and sports equipment to buy.

I thought I looked splendid in my bright blue blazer with silver grey edging, whereas my friends who went to Leyton High School looked very dull in comparison, with their drab grey blazers with red edging. When I was due to start, the school building in Nevin Drive, Chingford had not yet been finished, so school opened at Hawkwood House, a large Elizabethan-styled, Victorian mansion in the Yardley Hills. It was about a 15-minute walk from the nearest bus stop, or a slightly longer walk from Chingford Station.

I used to catch the number 38 bus from the Baker's Arms at Leyton. This worked very well for my first year at Chingford County High School, except on one cold, icy morning, when the bus could not get up Chingford Mount. The weather meant the bus stopped at the bottom of the hill, and we had to walk up the Mount to catch another bus and complete the journey to Chingford. I don't suppose they gritted the road in those days because there were too few motor vehicles to justify it.

My first year at the school was difficult for me academically. My strong, cockney accent was one problem, with my lack of discipline with homework another. The teaching staff comprised of four teachers and a headmaster for 65 pupils. The headmaster was called Mr Burdett. Our form teacher was called Mr Glover, who taught all the 'art' subjects, while Miss Noakes did all the maths, and science subjects. According to the school magazine, the science subjects were taught in the living room of the old house. I excelled at the 'arts' subjects and struggled with the maths and sciences, which is strange given my subsequent career as an electrical engineer!

The first major event of 1939 was the birth of my sister, Patricia Iris, on the 5th of March. I was   surprised when the Midwife came into my bedroom, gave me my breakfast and told me to get dressed. Pop gave me a letter to give to my Grandad and money for the tram. He told me not to worry about mum, as she was OK. 'Your Grandad will explain', Pop must have said. I certainly did not know she was pregnant! I wonder, how could I have been so unobservant? For some reason, neither Mum nor Pop, had ever told me. But I never lived my surprise down. Patsy, as we called her,

The Prosser Outing. *Grannie and Grandad are near the end at the right next to Flossie. Nellie, holding a baby which may be me) is next to Grandad. Sarah is in a dark coat next to me. Annie is next to and higher than her. Lizzie is next and also in a dark coat and next to a baby held by Jack. Eric is next to Jack with his arms around the lady at the left.   The lady behind the two men is Rose. Mum is next to Jack above the baby.   The man with Glasses at the top is Tommy.   The tall man in the back row is Bill Gillingham who was married to Nellie.   Joan, Joyce and someone else are the children at the front*

was a bonny baby and greatly admired in the Prosser and Mosley Families.

Then the second major event of 1939 was the war. It all began on Sunday, 3rd of September 1939, when Neville Chamberlain, our Prime Minister, declared war on Germany.

THE WAR

(1939–1942)

Sunday, 3rd of September was a lovely sunny day. Pop and Mum got me up early because of the imminent threat of War. All children in the London area were being offered evacuation. Mum said I was lucky because the whole of my school was being evacuated together. In total, 22 boys and 26 girls from school were evacuated. That Sunday morning, Mum and I had to get to school by 11am. We had to walk as the 38 did not run on a Sunday morning. The baby was left with Pop.

Mum had also been offered evacuation for herself and Patsy, who was only 6 months old, with my school but had declined, preferring to stay with Pop. This decision turned out to be the right one because the expected Blitz did not begin for over a year.

Back on 3rd September 1939, Mum and I set off with all my belongings in a small attaché case, and began the long journey. We were lucky to be picked up by Derek Meakins' dad, who drove us to the school. Derek and I had already decided that we wanted to be billeted together. When we arrived at our destination, the headmaster informed everybody that Neville Chamberlain, the Prime Minister, had announced that we were now at war with Germany. As young boys, we did not take it very seriously, we thought it would be over in a few weeks. The headmaster also told us that he had no idea where we were being evacuated to, but we were promised that it would be a safe location.

Shortly after 1 o'clock, the double-decker buses arrived and all 70 of us were driven off to an unknown location. Some of the girls were in tears, but I thought it would be like a holiday with my newly acquired brother, Derek. Later that afternoon we arrived in a high street, which was later identified as Billericay, in Essex, where ladies of the W.V.S (Women's Voluntary Service) looked after us. We were given emergency rations: tea, cocoa, biscuits, chocolate bar, corned beef etc. in a brown carrier bag. Sadly, most of the goodies were intended for our potential hostesses. We, however, made short work of the chocolate and biscuits we found in the bag.

On we went until we arrived at the car park of the Grand Spa hotel in the village of Hockley, Essex. We all went to the village hall, where we met the families who would be looking after us. Our billets had been previously allocated.

Derek and I were to be hosted by Mr and Mrs Bradley in their bungalow called 'Milverton' in Bramerton Road opposite the Congregational Church which would be our new school. The church had recently been built and was not fully completed, nor would it be until long after the war was over. It was made of wood and the photograph shows a much modernised building.

There were to be two classrooms, one for the 1938 intake which included me and Derek, and one for the 1939 intake. Given the circumstances, the syllabus was much reduced, we no longer had facilities such as laboratories, woodworking and metalworking workshops, and foreign language lessons all stopped. There was no playground or sports field, so we had to do our physical education in the classroom. The classrooms were only separated by sheets and curtains. Despite the circumstances, I remember these as happy times for us at the school, and our billet hosts were kind to us. We later found out that our headmaster, Mr Burdett had worked hard to make sure the entire school was kept together during the evacuation.

This was a period later called "the phony war", when nothing appeared to be happening in a warlike manner. However, after the passing of several months, the air raid sirens did eventually begin to sound often at night. Ironically, we would hear them from our makeshift beds under the stairs while our parents back in Leyton would sleep undisturbed. The reason for this, was that German aircraft were busy laying magnetic mines in the Thames estuary, often near Southend.

On my Birthday 1st October 1939, Mrs Bradley took us on a visit to nearby Southend, where we went to Garrons Cinema to see 'Beau Geste', a French Foreign Legion drama starring Brian Donlevy. While there, we had fish and chips followed by an ice cream, for which Southend was famous.

Suddenly, as we were walking down to the pier, the anti-aircraft guns on the end of the Pier (the longest in Britain), opened up on a very low-flying aircraft, which had obviously been laying mines. As it flew away, one of its engines was emitting large quantities of smoke, and everyone cheered. I remember that I later identified it as a Blohm & Voss flying boat. We may never know if it got home but, at the time, we all hoped that it didn't.

Yet despite these indications of war, London was still not being targeted, and so I was able to go home at Christmas. I went home on my own on the train. Mum and Pop were still in Leyton, but moved after Christmas because Pop's sister, Becky, was pregnant and wanted extra space. So they moved down the road to 26, James Lane. I never visited there as they soon moved to Surbiton and then Guildford. I never saw Auntie Becky or Uncle Ted again after Christmas 1939.

After a few days in Leyton, I returned to Hockley. Later, when fighting flared up in France, we had to leave the Bradley's as they had heard that their only son Ronald, a member of the Army Cycle Corps, had been reported missing, and Mrs Bradley was too ill with worry. So Derek and I had to move but, sadly, we could not move together, and I found myself living with Mr and Mrs Richardson, in another bungalow, ironically called 'The Bungalow', in White Hart Lane, in the nearby village of Hawkwell. They were a really nice couple who looked after me as if I were their own son.

My first night there had its surprises, as when I went to put my clothes in the wardrobe in my room, I found Mr. Richardson's artificial leg propped up in the corner. I found out later that he had lost his leg in the First World War, and had hated the Germans ever since. They had no children but once again, they were kind people who looked after us very well.

By this time, the war was going badly in Europe. The Germans had bypassed the Maginot Line and pushed south through Belgium, which quickly surrendered, leaving the British Expeditionary Force (BEF) in a precarious position. The situation got even worse when Marshall Petain surrendered all Northern France to the Germans, retaining limited control in Southern France in a puppet state that became known as Vichy France. The British Government fell and the National Government with a new Prime Minister, Winston Churchill, was established. Even as young children, we realised the gravity of this news.

The BEF then found themselves alone in their fight against superior German forces. They fell back in full retreat to Dunkirk on 26th of May 1940. All seemed lost, but then a miracle occurred, when 350,000 British, French and Belgian troops trapped on the beach, were saved by a fleet of hundreds of little ships. These vessels, owned by ordinary people, crossed the Channel at great personal risk to help evacuate the stranded army back to Southern England. Winston Churchill had only been the Prime Minister for nine days when this happened, but he refused to surrender. He was an excellent and stirring speaker, and rapidly becoming a great orator, who despite this defeat inspired the nation never to surrender. We listened to his speeches avidly on the radio.

Despite this feat of heroism, we all felt that Britain was now left alone to fight the war and that it was only a matter of time before the Germans would invade. Our army was in a bad way. The vast majority of its tanks, guns and ammunition had been left behind in France. While the army was hastily reorganized and re-equipped, we had to rely on our Navy and the RAF to keep the enemy at bay. The teachers and the adults tried to keep the worst news from us, but my friends and I were always convinced we would win.

The Government set up a 10-mile Coastal defence zone and, therefore, we could no longer stay in Hockley. Our school was evacuated again in the week after Dunkirk - this time to Coleford in the Forest of Dean, in the West Country, far from France. So it was time to say goodbye to Hockley and hello to Coleford. Many pupils, including Derek, went home rather than join us in Coleford. It was another 60 years before I saw him again.

Our journey from Hockley was a long one. We left at about 8 a.m. and arrived at Lydney, Gloucestershire, at about 8 p.m. We had been given nothing to eat or drink on the train beyond a glass of water at Cambridge and Birmingham stations. These stops also provided much needed toilet breaks, as we were travelling on a non-corridor train, which had no toilets.

When we reached Lydney, we were shown into a large Hall where we thought 'food at last'! But no, we were all medically examined before being bundled onto buses to Coleford. On arrival, we were ferried into another big hall, where we were all lined up to be picked out by prospective billet host or hostesses.

Peter Lines and I had chosen to be billeted together. Peter was a Dr Bernardo's Boy and, I now realise, he, like Derek, filled the gap I always wanted a brother to fill. I remember we waited nervously to be picked. Naturally, all the girls went first, as people assumed that they would be less trouble and more useful than the single boys. As two boys we were particularly difficult to house, but eventually a church minister, Rev. E.R. Vaughan and his wife, came and chose us. When we got back to 'the Manse' we were joined by an older couple, and it was explained to us that one of us would be staying at the Manse and the other with the older couple, Mr and Mrs Nash, who lived next door.

Mr and Mrs Nash chose me, while Peter was to live with the Rev. Vaughan and family. The selection may have been the other way around, but I do remember later that, in a letter to my mum, Mrs Nash said that she had chosen me because I looked angelic. On the first night with them, they cooked me a hearty meal and set up a camp bed for me to sleep in, in their sitting room. I was moved upstairs on the next night, and was delighted to find out that I had a smashing bedroom all to myself again.

Mr and Mrs Nash were retired grocers. He managed a lovely garden, and she was an amateur herbalist who had an herbal answer ready for all ailments. She was a good cook and looked after me well. However, she did not enjoy good health, so it did not surprise me when I was asked to move next door to be reunited with Peter with Mr and Mrs Vaughan and their son Bernard.

Peter and I were told to report to the Bells Grammar School in Coleford. While this school was founded in the 16th century, my school was not even two years old. What a difference! Our classes were to be housed in the host school's gymnasium and divided into two groups. There was another change of staff at the school. Miss Boagey taught French and Music. Miss Wyatt (Daisy) taught English, History and Geography.

As we now had limited access to the Chemistry and Physics laboratories for the first time since I joined the school in 1938, we were able to enjoy different content in our school curriculum. We all thought that the Bells Grammar School staff were good to us in allowing us to use their gym. Relations between the students of both schools were good too, and we

Congregational Church, Hockley

quickly adjusted to this new way of school life.

We were also encouraged to take a greater interest in the Coleford Congregational Church. We three boys: Bernard, Peter and I took over the pumping of the church organ, not only for the two main church services each Sunday but also for the choir and organ rehearsal sessions. Mrs Morse, the organist, sometimes needed our vigorous pumping effort - especially when she was rehearsing on her own. On one occasion, I accidentally stopped pumping and she was very annoyed! We also became members of the church choir and Christian Endeavour, which met every Thursday. We would have spelling bees, and other educational activities.

With our bikes, we often went to places of interest in the Forest of Dean - especially to Symonds Yat, where you could see the River Wye twisting and turning below. I started saving stamps because we had a stamp club at school. I remember it with fondness as a good time of my life. Surrounded by friends, we were never hungry, and the war felt like it was far away.

By some miracle or feat of skill and bravery on the part of the RAF, we were never invaded. The defeat of the Luftwaffe by the RAF in the Battle of Britain left a strong image in my consciousness about the bravery of RAF pilots. But before this victory, there were some worrying times, where we didn't know which way the war would go. The Germans were trying to starve us out by using their U-boats to sink our merchant ships, and many British cities were mercilessly blitzed by German bombers. London, in particular, was badly damaged and thousands of people, killed.

Of course, we missed our homes and family, particularly as the Blitz developed. At school, we were encouraged to write home. I was particularly worried about my Grannies and Grandads.

I did not go back home for Christmas 1940 because the Blitz was at its height. Mum told me that Grannie and Grandad Prosser were OK in the letters she wrote to me. To stay safe, they went into a large, nearby, communal brick shelter because Grandad could not manage the walk to Old Street Underground Station. They went every night from 4 p.m. until 8 a.m. They were near the heart of the Blitz because they lived near the train stations, the City and not far from the Docks in the East End. When the Blitz began in earnest, Pop's firm 'Lovell and Christmas', based at Smithfield, were evacuated to Berrylands, Surbiton, and then, when the Blitz got worse, they were moved again to Aldershot Road, Guildford. There, they found accommodation for Mum and Pop in a flat in a newly built house in Hillview Crescent, just opposite the newly acquired warehouse where Pop was to work. This house was where Mum lived until she died in 1999. Kevin was born here when my wife and lived in the upstairs flat and Stephen later on bought the house.

Back to 1940, there was a lull in the bombing over Christmas, which allowed us to go home. We travelled back home via the Red and White Coach Service from Gloucester. During this brief period, I visited Grannie and Grandad and saw their air raid shelter. I thought it was pretty grim, crowded, undecorated and dirty, but they regarded it as a great place of safety. They used to go into the Shelter at 4pm in the Winter and 8pm in the summer.

The war dragged on through, and we had the sense that it would never end. The period of heavy bombing came to an end in May 1941 as the Luftwaffe was withdrawn to fight on the Eastern Front. In December of the same year, the Japanese Navy attacked Pearl Harbour with great force and destroyed the US Pacific Fleet, killing thousands of people. Franklin D. Roosevelt, the US President, immediately declared war on Japan and its allies Germany and Italy.

This was a tremendous boost to us in Britain because we had been the only country in Europe still fighting the Germans and Italians, and now we had a powerful new ally in the US.

What we did not know at that time was that there would be widespread invasions of British Colonies such as Hong Kong, Singapore and Burma to come. The Americans would be engaged in many, many battles in the Pacific, stretching from Hawaii to Japan itself.For us on our tiny Island, there was a feeling that while we were not 'out of the woods yet by a long chalk', we were no longer alone!

At school every morning, we were given a third of a pint of milk and a Crookes Halibut Oil capsule as a supplement to our diet. My health was good; I rarely had a cough or cold. I did a lot of cycling and walking. I enjoyed singing both at school and at the church. On one of my school reports, Miss Boagey described me as an enthusiastic and talented singer. On the same report, my headmaster, Mr Burdett, said that my voice, not the softest in the class, was heard far too often.

At one of my Christian Endeavour meetings, I met a pretty young girl named Winnie Pocket, who normally lived at Chapel-en-la-Frith in Derbyshire. She had been evacuated to live with her grandmother further down Gloucester Road from 'The Manse' where I lived. She later became my first girlfriend and part of the same church group of young people as Peter, Bernard and I. I was recently reminded of her when I found my first autograph book, which I was given in early 1942, as it contains several references to her.

Our church choir was invited to take part in Handel's Messiah at Gloucester Cathedral as part of the Free Churches Choir Festival. The conductor was to be Adrian Bolt, a very famous conductor, who conducted at the Royal Opera House and Diaghilev's ballet company. He was also Director of Music at the BBC and the London Philharmonic Orchestra. While he would conduct the actual performance, at the rehearsals we had the conductor of the BBC Symphony Orchestra, Patrick Jenkins, presiding. It was a great experience, and today Handel's Messiah remains my favourite piece of music. It was played at our wedding and at my wife, Jean's, funeral.

After a short Christmas holiday, I returned to Coleford where some of my fellow pupils who lived in Chingford reported that the new school buildings had been completed, and that our past Deputy

Headmistress, Miss Noakes, was to be in charge of the 1941 intake. As things were quiet with regard to air raids in Chingford, some of the parents started pressing for us to move back home at the end of the summer term in 1942. I was very unhappy with this decision as Mum and Pop had moved to Guildford, and I would have to leave Chingford County High School, to go to Surrey, many miles away. My mum knew this and tried to make arrangements for me to stay with one of her many sisters for what was to be my last year at school. But the air raid attacks (VI and V2) began again so that it was not a possible solution.

So it was to be goodbye, Coleford. Goodbye, Mr & Mrs Vaughan and Bernard. Goodbye to Mr and Mrs Nash. Goodbye, Coleford Congregational Church; Bells Grammar School; Winnie; and goodbye Peter, who I would never see again. He was a good pal. Nor would I see Bernard Vaughan again, but I did see his parents, Mr and Mrs Vaughan again and Winnie as I went back to Coleford again in 1946 when I was in the RAF. Sadly, both Mr and Mrs Nash had passed away.

Hello Guildford. Hello Mum, Pop and Patsy, I am on my way!

GUILDFORD/WOKING
(1942–1945)

Jean, Sandy and I, 1948

When I came home from Coleford to 2, Hillview Crescent, all the family were pleased to see me. Mum had put my bed in the sitting room, together with a chest of drawers for my clothes. Patsy had her own bed in the bedroom with Mum and Pop. They had the downstairs floor, while the upstairs was occupied by the manager of the firm Pop worked for.

Patsy loved having her big brother around, and everywhere I went in the flat, she would follow. She was a bright and bonnie three-year-old with blonde hair. I soon got to know Pop's workmates, especially a young driver called Pete Monroe, who took me out in his lorry delivering the food that was still on ration.

Dad's firm used to deliver ham, sides of beef, lamb, kippers, butter and cheese. They were wholesale, so they delivered to shops like Sainsbury's and other retail grocers.

As all the schools were closed for the summer holidays, I could do little to get a place at the local grammar school for my last year at school. Mr Burdett had sent a sealed reference letter, and Mum arranged for me to be interviewed at the Royal Grammar School in Guildford and the Woking Boys Grammar School as soon as both schools reopened after the summer holidays.

Mum took me to these interviews, but they felt very different from any I had experienced before. At the Royal Grammar School, as soon as the headmaster read Mr Burdett's letter, he listed all my deficiencies, and we were out of the door quickly. At Woking, I was whisked away and given a wide-ranging verbal examination and then ferried back to my mum for the decision. The teacher thought that I had done very well, but would be unable to get up to the standard required to successfully pass the School Certificate. This required the student to pass in six subjects, including English and Maths. The teacher felt that it would be better for me to get a job, while I worked out what I wanted to do with my life, and then study as appropriate at evening class. I did do this, on his advice, when I took a shorthand and typing course at Clarke College, Guildford. But I gave it up as a bad job after only 2 weeks because I was uninterested in a secretarial career.

A few weeks later, our next door neighbour, Mr. Palmer, who was project manager at Warner Engineering offered me a job as a trainee in the

Engineering Department. As part of my induction I was first taught to be competent in the use of basic hand tools such as the file, hacksaw and hand drill. Then encouraged to further develop my skills on various machines, such as lathes, mills and heat treatment tools. I accepted and that is where I worked for the next 6 months.

I found the work boring and repetitive, but I found a new friend in Bernard (Bun) Henderson, who was a fellow trainee. I was at that time a member of the Guildford Army Cadets Corps, but Bun persuaded me to join the Woking 1349 Squadron Air Training Corps (ATC), and to become a trumpeter in their band. Bun played the side drum, but then there was no vacancy for a drummer. I used to go over to Bun's on Saturday morning, stay over on Saturday night, and then go to the ATC on Sunday morning. But I'd always be back home to have my Sunday lunch with my family.

I became more and more interested in 1349 Squadron, ATC, and enjoyed my efforts as trumpeter in the band. There were six side drummers, a bass drummer called Morrie Burchett and eight trumpeters. Leading the band was a man called Nobby Hobbs, who was the Drum Major. Our trumpets were E flat Valveless Trumpets. We practised on Sundays in the school playground at Goldsworth Road Infant School, near where we later lived, and my children went to school. We also had a Nissen Hut (a pre-fabricated corrugate iron hut with a semicircular roof used through-out the war). This is where we had our meetings and lessons. Today, the Surrey History Centre stands on the site where the ATC Nissen hut once stood.

About once a month, the band used to parade through the streets of Woking, going as close as we could to the Drill Hall in Walton Road where the Woking Army Cadets bugle band was housed. We wanted to show them how good we were! The trumpets were not played all the time, unlike the drums. I don't think any of the band could read music, instead we played by ear. When we approached the centre of Woking, we would play three marching tunes. These would be selected by Bo Stanley, the leading trumpeter, at the appropriate moment. Mossie Burchett would give four beats on the bass drum, and this would be the signal for the trumpets to sound. When we finished our marching tunes, this too would be signalled by two double beats on the bass drum.

The lessons I attended at the ATC comprised Navigation, Aircraft Recognition, Stars and Planets. We also had a football team which played other ATC teams. We were quite successful in our footballing efforts – we were the losing finalists in the two full seasons that I played - eventually losing to Kingston and Wimbledon. I played at left-half because the coach thought I was too one-sided on the right side, and thought it would be good for the team on the left.

We used to have annual camps where we camped in a school or college when they were on their summer vacations and visited nearby RAF units. The venue I remember most clearly was Birchington in Kent, where we spent some time at sea with the RAF Search and Rescue Unit. We also went to the Coastal Command RAF base at Holmsley South in the New Forest, where I was offered a trip to the Azores in a US Navy Liberator, which I had to refuse. This was typical of the

American approach to life, offering such a trip in the middle of the war. I did, however, accept a return flight to Roose Airport in Wales, which, I believe, is the present Cardiff Airport. It was in an Avro York, a transport variant of the Avro Lancaster Bomber. I thoroughly enjoyed my time in the ATC, and I think I made a favourable impression.

Our training with the ATC was regularly monitored by the President, Mr Fitzroy Woods. At one of my monitoring interviews, Mr Woods questioned me about my employment with Warner Engineering. I told Mr Woods that I was very bored with the work I was doing, filing, drilling, polishing items, but they were helping our war effort. Mr Woods then offered me a job as a trainee draughtsman - I would be trained as a cartographic draughtsman first and then as an architectural draughtsman later.

So I joined WESCO (Woking Electric Supply Company)in the spring of 1943. I was told to report to the Commissionaire at their works in Walton Road, Woking, the next Monday morning. What happened in the first 5 minutes of that first day would eventually mean a terrific change in my life.

On my first day at WESCO. I reported to Frank Bennion, the Commissionaire, at 8am as ordered. I was to go upstairs to the main office, turn right and go to the far end where there were two large drawing boards. I was to wait until 9am for Mr Didcot to come in.

Our circle of friends in the Woking Era - From the left Barbara and Ken Turner; Jean; Derek and Lorna Smith; Bun and Dot Henderson; Bob and Ester Lambert c1960

When I went into the main office, I was amazed at this huge room, which was 50 feet long, 25 feet wide, and 15 foot high and yet empty except for one young girl. Again, as instructed, I walked to the far end of the office and waited for my new boss to appear. The girl then went out of the office, leaving me on my own for ages. When she returned, she saw me sitting on a stool and came down to me and said 'You can't sit on that stool, that's where Mr Didcot sits, you have to sit on the other stool'.

That was my first meeting with Jean Engall, aged 14-years-old, who became my wife five years later on 10th April 1948. Much later, Jean reminded me that I had said to her on that first day "Thank you, Miss Bossy Boots'. Our Daughter Kathryn would, much later, inherit this same title. Jean was always a 'happy-go-lucky' girl. We started to go out with each together eventually, 18 months later, but more of that anon.

A strange arrangement existed at WESCO in that all the under 21-year-olds (under the age of consent) started work at 8am, and all adult employees would start at 9am. All the manual workers had to 'clock' in and out, but all technical and administrative staff came and went without any obvious check.

There was very little work done by the 'kids' between 8 and 9am. We all congregated in the meter test office and generally 'messed about' - swapping sweets/chocolates (both rationed) until 8.45am. Out of my wages I bought a drawing set and a box of 'French Curves' which were templates of a whole range of curves which you could trace round when you were doing a technical drawing.

My boss, Tim Didcot, was the Chief Draughtsman and he and I were the drawing office (D.O). Before the war, there were three other staff in the D.O. The most senior was Ernie Goater, now in the Army, then Eric Hunter and John Moffat both in the RAF. I never thought about it then, but looking back, my employment prospects at the end of the war were doubtful.

My first big job was to print out onto linen, a complete set of the 10KV, 2KV, and 200 volt cable records which were then put into fireproof boxes and stored in the big brick storage area of the shop in Chobham Road, Woking. It was felt that this was necessary to create an alternative set in case of fire destroying the cable records stored in the D.O. If there was a cable fault, you need the cable records to be able to see where the cables were.

The Drawing Office. I'm second on the left.

From that time, we were starting to get a big military build-up of British and Canadian troops for the Invasion (D-Day) both at the Inkerman barracks at Knaphill and the large army camp at Pirbright. A huge area of Ottershaw, Longcross, and Chertsey Common were given over to a massive army vehicles car park so that all the vehicles could park under trees to hide them from aerial observation.

During 1944/45, I had to go out much more on my bike to take records of any cable laying or alterations. I used to use my bike, but only in the Woking area. For trips further afield, I used to cadge a lift with the mains or commercial engineers. This arrangement was rapidly becoming impossible and made even worse when the company issued a new two-part tariff with a fixed tariff for domestic and light commercial industrial consumers. My friend, Derek Smith and I, were assessors of these tariffs.

The fixed part of this tariff was assessed domestically by the total area of the house or flat, with a minimum of 800 square feet. Commercial industrial tariffs were based on installed electrical loads. The charge was three-quarter pence per unit (a kilowatt-hour). This tariff became very popular, and as the assessor, I had to become more mobile as I had more customers to deal with. Management decided that the Street Lighting motorbike and sidecar, which had been idle since the outbreak of war, should be made available to me after suitable training. This training consisted of going round and round the cable drum and transformer store until Jimmy Dallen, the Garage Foreman, decided that I could drive the motorbike and sidecar OK. We affixed a set of ladders on the top of the sidecar. I applied for a provisional licence, as there were no driving tests during the War – and, when this was granted, I became the regular and only driver of a BSA 500 cc side valve motorbike and a box sidecar. This was exactly the same as the yellow AA outfit that provided the first motor breakdown service for motorists in Great Britain. (n.b. I have held a driving licence for many years, but have still never had a formal driving test).

You may well ask 'why did I still carry the heavy double section wooden ladder on the top of the sidecar'? Every time the rider negotiated a left-hand bend, the sidecar wheel tended to lift and the driver and pillion passenger had to lean to the left to counter this. The heavy ladder helped weigh the sidecar down and was a great help. But when I was a more experienced driver, the ladder was no longer necessary. This experience was useful when Jean and I had a sidecar for my Ariel 500cc Red Hunter motorbike after Stephen was born in 1951.

When the ATC found out that I could ride a motorcycle and sidecar, I was told to go with Mr Osland (sorry, Flying Officer Osland) to Fairoaks Airport at Chobham, where the ATC had opened a gliding centre. In this centre, there were two gliders: a fairly new Kirby Kadet, and an ancient Dagline. There was also a Rolls-Royce Essex Car, which had been converted to a flat bedded glider retrieval vehicle and a 988cc Zenith motorbike and sidecar, which was used to retrieve the winch tow-rope and help launch the gliders.

The motorbike was an old 'belt' drive, which today would be worth a fortune. It was more difficult to drive than the BSA, due to the 'belt' replacing the 'chain'. For example, when the grass was dry, when you opened the throttle, the 'belt' would almost straight away react like the 'chain'. When wet, you would lurch forward alarmingly, as the 'belt' would not move the bike until it had completely dried out.   You would then put the bike into 'neutral,' attach the tow-rope to the bike, then drive off to the take-off point where you would take the tow-rope off the bike and attach it to the glider to launch it.

Fairoaks was a RAF Basic Pilot Training Unit and all its aircraft were De Haviland Tiger Moths. This centre had been vital in the early days of the Battle of Britain, when we were always short of fighter pilots. But it had maintained its usefulness, particularly as we were suffering large losses of air-crew with the almost nightly attacks on Germany and German held territories.

In the early part of 1943, Pop started having violent headaches, for which he could get little relief. Pop had fallen off a lorry a short while before and hurt his head, so his manager at work decided to have him referred to a specialist in Harley Street. I think, in hindsight, that Mum should have gone with him. A workmate, called Reg Best, went with him instead. As a result, Mum was never given any specific diagnosis, and he continued to have very painful attacks. These were beginning to have marked side effects. I learned, much later, that Mum would take a hammer to bed with her to protect Patsy. This, thank God, was never necessary.

Pop eventually went into a coma, and he was taken to the Surrey County Hospital in Farnham Road. Mum went to see him as often as she could, but Patsy and I were only allowed to visit on Sunday afternoons and even then, we were only allowed in for a few minutes, one at a time, as they were very strict about the two visitors rule and not sitting on the bed.

I don't think Pop ever regained consciousness, and he died peacefully in his sleep. He was only 43, and Mum was 41. So, for the second time in her life, Mum became a widow, and I lost another father. Pop was laid to rest in the cemetery at Stoke, in Guildford.

Money was going to be a problem again, but as I was now earning a wage, and I was paying Mum a weekly rent, things were not too bad. Patsy was now in the same position I had been when I lost my dad, but with one huge difference. In my case, all of my mum's sisters and cousins lived locally, and we saw them regularly. But now we were in Guildford, none of them were anywhere near us, so Patsy was robbed of contact with her many cousins, aunts and uncles.

1944 was the year of the opening of the Second Front. The memory of D-Day and the beginning of the liberation of Western Europe leading to the defeat of the Fascists armies, and the end of Hitler and Mussolini, will remain in my memory forever.

Britain continued the bombing of Germany, Italy and the unfortunate countries that were occupied by the enemy. The US Air Force bombed Germany during the day with their Flying Fortresses and Liberator Bombers. While the RAF hammered them by night with their Lancaster and Halifax bombers. We were now having 1,000 aero craft bomber raids by the RAF but with very high casualty rates.

The fortunes of this country and its allies greatly improved during the year of 1944. The U-boat threat was receding faster than we had ever expected. Our Navy now dominated the seas. There was a massive build-up of men and materials needed to beat Germany. This built up to a climax on June 6[th,] 1944.

Our ATC summer camp this year was held at Birchington High School, where the highlight was our day out with the Air Sea Rescue Unit at Ramsgate. The weather was terrible, and as there was no prospect of any enemy attacks, we put to sea. A one-man dinghy had been cast into the sea earlier in the day about two miles out from the coast, and it was our job, in the air-sea rescue launch, to locate the dinghy and bring the pilot (a dummy) back.

Our officer, Bob Beldam, went down with seasickness and I replaced him in the port-side observation turret. It was pouring with rain. There was a very heavy swell and visibility was poor. After a long time searching, we gave up and went back to Ramsgate. It was lucky I was protected from the worst of the weather. It was an exciting day and not one I will forget. The poor dummy, unfortunately, was lost at sea!

Later in the year, I started to go out with Jean. The early problem was that she was already going out with Roy Smith - a 19-year-old who was a regular with the RAF. She just said she would give him up so that we could go out to the pictures and dances together. Jean's family were avid film goers and went to the pictures three times a week, but only when Pop (Jean's dad) was on the early or night shift. He was a fireman and assistant engine driver at Guildford station on the Southern Railway.

At home, Patsy started school. Mum started to cook at Hadley's, where they made spectacle frames in its factory in Portsmouth Road, Guildford. She soon made friends with Lillian Bartlett and Elsie White. To reinforce a very restricted diet amid food shortages, Mum started keeping rabbits. These multiplied quickly, and one of Pop's friends used to kill them for us. We had to keep this from Patsy who frequently played with, and loved the 'wabbits'.

At work, I would have my dinner (now called lunch) in the British Restaurant in Chapel Street in Woking. The meal cost 6 old pence, 3d main course, 2d afters. 1d tea (nicknamed Rosie Lee in cockney rhyming slang). The restaurants were run by the Women's Voluntary

Service during wartime. The meal was really filling, and it helped to make our rations go further at home.

I used to cycle to work and then use the motorbike at work to get around. I was working in Woking on two things: cable records and the all-in-one standing charge assessments. During the war there was little work on

Jean's Mum and Dad - Percy and May Engall, Jean and me. c1948-9

cable records because so few new cables were being laid, but this dramatically increased from 1946 onwards. It was important because the cable position had to be located quickly in case of a fault.

Sometime in 1944, I was given the assistance of John Matthews, a tiny 14-year-old of 5ft 5in. He soon developed into a strapping lad of 6 foot 4 in. (He retired, after a career as an administrator, to Barnstaple in Devon, and we are still in touch.)

As well as our normal jobs, we were given the informal task of preparing the theatre (which was upstairs in our building) for dances and whist drives. We used to wax and polish the floor. Many of the dances were put on especially for the troops. They were usually held on Friday or Saturday night, and the bakers used to send in large trays of free pastries and soft drinks. Some of which, John and I raided as a reward for our effort!

I spent many weekends in Woking. In the winter, Bun and I, along with a group of friends, often went over to Aldershot Town FC to watch their home games. During the war the Football League was suspended, so many of the Country's best players, who were in the Army, were in the Aldershot team. They, in fact, had the England team's half back line with Britten, Cullis, and Mercer. Stan Cullis was the England Captain, and Joe Mercer, much later becoming an Arsenal player, captain and manager with Manchester City (and, for a short time, England Manager).

After the match, we usually went back to Woking to prepare for a dance or some other form of entertainment. Occasionally, we stayed on to go to Aldershot Hippodrome to see a variety show. A group of us were once ejected for throwing back on stage small carrots and Brussels sprouts, which had been lobbed at the audience during a comedy dance.

Sunday mornings were spent at ATC meetings – rehearsal for the band (we were excused square bashing) and lessons on aircraft recognition and navigation. During this year, I became the leading trumpeter, and occasionally played the Last Post & Reveille at the RAF section of Brookwood Cemetery, which was one of the main war cemeteries. The highpoint of my musical career was on November 11th 1945 (the first Armistice Day of peacetime), when I played the Last Post and Reveille with the Central Band of the RAF. It was broadcast on the Home Service of the BBC!

I assumed the professionals were going to play it. Our branch of the ATC was presented with a Silver Trumpet for musical services during the War, and to my surprise our C.O. gave it to me and asked me to play the Last Post & Reveille on it. I told him it was too cold to play, so I played on my ordinary Trumpet and was broadcast by the BBC. When I got home, Mum said she had heard it but told me that I normally played it much better!

At home, Jean's paternal grandmother (her Dad's Mum) owned a removals firm, "Engall's Removals" from her home and depot in Boundary Road. She also had a small warehouse for furniture and storage. Pop's younger brother Fred ran the business, often with Pop's help.

I started to look after the garden at the front of my Mum's House at 2 Hillview Crescent. We had a large front garden but only a tiny triangular garden at the back. I grew potatoes and cabbage. The soil was solid grey clay, which was very difficult to dig. I double dug it, and it gradually got easier, but we never got it into a condition where it would accept seeds. The results, however, were remarkable. The cabbages were huge – we had an all-out war on the snails and slugs, who appeared out of nowhere in the autumn after it rained a lot following a lovely warm summer. The potatoes, which were Ulster Chieftains, were delicious, and we had a good crop. I kept it up the next year until I went into the RAF in January 1946. A question I am often asked is: 'was I hungry during the war?', and I can honestly say no! Although I did miss my sweets and chocolate because they were put on ration.

These years had a marked significant change in my life; moving from London to Guildford and Woking, Patsy's dad passing away and Patsy starting school. Little did I realise that 1945 would completely alter everyone's life here and all over the world.

FLEET AIR ARM?

(1945)

I'm on the left at St. Athans, S Wales

Early in 1945, I applied to the Royal Navy to become a trainee Pilot/Observer in the Fleet Air Arm. This was despite my inability to swim and great fear of the water - which I was hoping would dissolve when I was taught to swim by the Fleet Air Arm. Alas, this was not to be because I have still got the fear of water today. I went for interviews at Queen Anne Mansions in Westminster, where I had a very lengthy medical test, which I passed on condition that I would take an exacting eye test afterwards in Woking. However, I still had to pass the series of intelligence and aptitude tests that took place in the afternoon. This I did, and later I was also successful in the eye test, where I was found to have 60/60 vision. (we now tend to say 20/20 which is an American expression).

I was now a trainee Pilot/Observer with a Fleet Air Arm number and with instructions to report for duty at 10 a.m. 1st of October 1945 - my 18th birthday - to HMS Daedalus, a stonewalled frigate, at Gosport for basic training in Hampshire. A stonewalled frigate was slang for a land base which was given the rank of a frigate (a frigate is a small warship).

The war against the Germans continued to go well with General Eisenhower, an astute leader. Although it was generally accepted that Monty, the British Field Marshal, was giving him and the other Americans a hard time. In the Pacific, the American Navy and Marine Forces faced great resistance as they advanced bit-by-bit, suffering large casualties on land, sea and air. First, the Americans overwhelmed the Japanese Navy. This also destroyed the Japanese Air Force, as they were all carrier based. Our boys in the 14th Army, under General Bill Slim, often called the Forgotten Army, gradually pushed their wicked opponents out of Burma but still had to clear them out of Malaya and Singapore with the 'Japs' resisting hard all the way.

In Europe, the first country to fall to us was Italy after another long, hard-fought battle. Russian forces from the East and Anglo-American armies from the West fought onto German soil. When the Russians got to Berlin, Germany surrendered to Monty on Luneburg Heath on 4th May 1945. Hitler and his closest associates committed suicide.

At last, the War in Europe was over. This day would forever be known as VE day. Both my grandparents had survived the Blitz and only Uncle Charlie's (my dad's elder brother) two sons had lost their lives - Charlie died at Salerno and is buried near the beach in the war grave, and Jimmie died, aged 18, at the battle of Reichwald Forest, and is buried in the war grave in the forest. According to David Warren, who is now a battlefield tour guide, received information that Jimmie was reported by the Commanding Office as a typical bright Cockney lad.

Following the end of the war, we were then introduced to images of the emaciated prisoners in the recently freed concentration camps in the newspapers, and in the Pathé news broadcast at the cinema. The terrible news that the Nazis killed millions of Jews in an attempt to wipe out the Jewish race in occupied Europe, spread to a horrified world. This vile campaign is now known as the Holocaust, but is more precisely described as ethnic cleansing.

Then we received more news that shook the world. In August 1945, the Americans had dropped the atom bomb on Japan on Nagasaki and Hiroshima. Tens of thousands of Japanese civilians had been killed. The two large cities were destroyed. The Japanese Emperor immediately surrendered, and the final part of the war finished. This day is now known as VJ Day, signalling the end of the war in Burma, Malaya, Singapore and Hong Kong, and Japan.

Jean and I went up to London for VE Day and later also for the VJ Celebrations, where there was singing and dancing in the streets. We went by train to Waterloo, and then walked to Piccadilly. We went with our friends Esther and Bob. It was a great time.

News then filtered out about the dreadful treatment that troops suffered at the hands of the Japanese Army. However, it was peace at last.

On the Home Front, I was no longer wanted by the Fleet Air Arm, instead they offered me a short service commission as a trainee Pilot/Observer but only if I were willing to sign up for 10 years and for five more years in the Reserves. This had no attraction for me, as the war was over, and I did not want a career in any of the Armed Forces.

Immediately after I turned the Fleet Air Arm down, I received my National Service call-up papers for the Army! As a member of the ATC, I did not like this at all. So I went to the RAF recruitment office in Croydon and volunteered for the RAF. Luckily, the recruiting officer was willing to backdate my application. So, I said goodbye to the Fleet Air Arm, then to the Army, and hello to the RAF.

Jean came over to our house for Christmas 1945. We prepared the presents, and put them in the living room, where I was to sleep. Mum, Jean and Patsy slept in the bedroom. I acted as Father Christmas and tried to take the presents into Mum's bedroom, but several times got sent away as Patsy was still awake. Presents in those days were small, like chocolates, or ribbons, and fruit like oranges were put into the Christmas stocking.

Food was still rationed, and I can still remember Patsy's reaction when she first saw a banana. All the school children were given a banana, and she did not realise that the banana had to be peeled before she could eat it!

Christmas dinner was probably chicken, followed by Christmas Pudding, and Christmas Cake. My Mum was a great cook and we had a lovely feast. She used to put 'Silver Joeys' (these were threepennies) into the Pudding so that Patsy could find them. She continued this when my children, Stephen and Kevin, were born. Kevin reminds me that as soon as the children found them, she took the silver coins back and put them in a small brown envelope for use next year!

PEACE

(1946 - 1948)

I'm lying down at the bottom right. Metfield

Early in 1946 I received my call-up papers for the RAF.
I was to report to the Recruitment Centre at Padgate in
Lancashire. This is where I received my uniform after a
medical examination, and then there were a number of
intelligence/aptitude tests when they decided what trade
I would join. I tried to get Air Crew and while there
were no vacancies, I did have a wide group of trade
offers open to me. The group that I was interested in
was aircraft maintenance and repair, following in my
Dad's footsteps. However, before I could start, I had to
do my basic training. This was designed to get you fit,
and we did plenty of square-bashing or parade drills.
For this, they sent me to Metfield in Suffolk, which had
only very recently been made available to the RAF by
the American Army Air Force. In fact, it was so recent

a hand-over that whilst on picket duty, a coach rolled up packed with girls who were so disappointed by the lack of Americans that they got straight back on and returned to Ipswich! The motto of 'overpaid, oversexed, over here' certainly applied to these Americans in Suffolk.

We found out that Metfield had been a US Army Air Force Base, where two squadrons of Flying Fortresses operated from. In all the Nissen Huts, those with the semicircular roofs, the ceilings were completely covered with pin-up pictures. My bed was just feet away from the huge Crocodile Stove, round which every evening we all clustered - as it was warm.

Nissen Huts at Lasham

Looking back on my time at Metfield, I realised that I had enjoyed it very much. I was very fit and the 12 of us in our Nissen Hut had got on surprisingly well. We were a motley crew. There was Tom Shaughnissey (my best friend at Metfield) from Manchester, his dad was a Coal man who had a difficult time during the war as the country was so short of coal. Then there was Mark, a farmer's son from Westmorland, who was very religious and was up and dressed at 5 a.m. every morning. Ted Rubens, from Winchester, whose Dad sold motorcycles. Ted had his own motorbike, which he

wanted to bring to Metfield when he next had leave. His request was turned down, as we were only going to be at Metfield for a short time. We wondered where he was going to get petrol from because fuel was very difficult to get due to rationing - there was no petrol at all for private
motoring.

The main aim of these basic training courses, was to make you fit. So there was plenty of physical and endurance exercises as well as parade drills. To our surprise, one hanger had been turned into a gymnasium, with a boxing ring at one end. All the physical exercise was done indoors, and all the endurance exercises outside in the freezing cold. The USAF must have had this work done as the RAF were much too mean.

We had a surprise on our first parade when Freddie Mills, a famous boxer (who would go on to become the World Light Heavyweight Champion), turned out to be our physical training officer. He came with us on our first three-mile jog. While we ran, he cycled on his push-bike.

As part of our endurance training, we had to run the perimeter track, which was about 800 yards round. As we were there from January to March, we did this in the freezing cold. I found out that I was good at the 880 yards (half mile) run. So good, in fact, that I was given some middle distance running training. I even developed a sprint finish. Looking back on it. I wished I had kept it up!

At the end of the course, I was very surprised to be given the 'outstanding trainee' award, and an invitation to become an instructor at Metfield, with the rank of corporal. I was not excited by the idea, and quite surprised at the offer. When I told the officer of my decision not to stay, he appeared disappointed, but I have never regretted it since.

After saying our goodbyes, Tom and I were loaded down with our kit bags and dropped off at the nearest station, where we got on a train to Liverpool Street. On arrival in London, we decided to get a trolley bus to Paddington Station. This was more easily said than done, but Tom had never been to London before, and he wanted to see as much of it as he could. Looking back, the only difficult part of our journey from Metfield to Melksham was the middle bit of crossing London.

Melksham in Wiltshire was the Instrument Training Centre both for the RAF and the Fleet Air Arm. The two services were kept separate for training and accommodation, but we could see the different approaches to discipline that there was between the two forces. For example, in the Fleet Air Arm, punishment for an infringement was to dress in full uniform and pack, holding a rifle above the head and then run around the parade ground a number of times - dependent on the offence committed. There were no physical punishments in the RAF, they preferred fines and suspension of leave, and confinement to barracks. We only ever mixed with the Fleet Air Arm at the NAAFI (Navy, Army, Air force Institution), cinema and sports field.

Waiting to demob at St. Athans

The classes were small because there was a lot of bench work. Our course was for Instruments Repairers, Class 2. We concentrated on instruments that were in general use in the RAF. We did not get much practical work in things such as automatic pilots, gyro types of gun and bomb sights, but instead were given instructions on the inspection and maintenance of these types of equipment. The more complicated areas of work such as repairing and re-commissioning were covered in the Instrument Repairers Class 1 course.

We had most weekends free, but I could not afford to go home every week and Tom could not go home to Manchester at all because of the high travel costs and time it would take to get home. Even if he could afford it, most of the weekend would be spent on travelling. We used to go into Bristol for the Speedway once a week. This was not arranged by the RAF, but by one of the trainees on the course. I remember that the coaches involved were provided by Hatt's Coaches of Devizes. The driver, Nelson Hatt, son of the owner, said they also ran coaches to London.

These coaches were organised by one of the trainees (rewarded with a free seat). It was much cheaper than the rail fare from Melksham to Paddington. I did try it once, but it was too long a journey, so on the next Bristol Speedway night I asked Nelson whether his dad would consider running a small coach to Reading, and if so, how much would he charge? The answer came back that he would. I think the charge was £1. If I could get 15 people on the 20 seater coach, I would get the free seat. I had already gone round all the huts, and with Tom's help we soon had 12 names. But despite our efforts, we could only get 14 names, including mine. So I found myself having to pay for my seat after all. Subsequently, I resumed trying to get more names. Some of the lads who lived south of London, who had previously caught one of the London Coaches, decided to try ours instead, and from then on, I got my free seat for the rest of my time in Melksham.   From Reading, I could get the train to Guildford, and see Jean, Mum and Patsy.

Tom and I both passed the tests at the end of the course. I was then posted to Henlow in Hertfordshire as an instrument repairer, and Tom was posted to Aldergrove near Belfast in Northern Ireland. Although we never met again, we continued to correspond for some time.

RAF Henlow had been the RAF Apprentice School before the war. At the end of the war, they developed it into a fairly large Aerodrome. As Henlow was only a few miles from de Havilland's main aircraft factory at Radlett, we were the receiving airport for the aeroplanes made in the de Havilland's Canadian factory. The ferry pilots flew in all the Mosquitoes made in Canada. I was given the job of the daily inspection (all aircraft in the RAF were inspected daily using the Form 800) where any faults experienced by the ferry pilots were recorded.

I had quite a shock at my first inspection, as the plane's altimeter was not the usual barometric one but was an electric one, made by the Sperry company, a giant firm from the USA. The Engineering Officer and our section's 'Chiefy' (as all sergeants in the instrumental section of the RAF were known), were requesting help from the manufacturers.

Chiefy was missing the next morning but emerged later in the day with all the necessary paperwork and one of the new electric radio altimeters. This instrument was a major advance in RAF avionics. It turned out that he had gone to the American base at Mildenhall, where his opposite number gave him an instruction book and the altimeter to practice on. The American air force did not repair any instruments on-site – any faulty instruments would be returned to the manufacturers if repairable. It would be another five years before the RAF followed suit.

After I had been at Henlow for about six months, the Douglas DC-3 (Dakota) of the Air Chief Marshal, Lord Tedder flew in. The plane needed refurbishment, mainly in the interior but also the removal of the camouflage paint. After conducting the daily instrument checks, I spent the morning admiring the interior office and bedroom on the aeroplane.

While doing my checks, I noted that this aircraft had an American autopilot, so I rushed back to my billet to get the notes I had taken on autopilots during the Melksham course. I should have gone back to the instrument workshop and sought the help of a more experienced colleague, but as I was only doing the daily check, I decided to use my notes instead.

When back at the plane, I was using my notes as I removed the back of the control box. Whilst doing this, I became aware that I was being watched by an officer who asked me "What do you think you are doing?" to which I replied, "the daily inspection, sir!"

"Why do you need those notes then?" he said, to which I replied: "because I have never done an inspection of an autopilot before, sir!"

"Pass me your notes" he said, and then looked all through my notes and when finished gave the books back and walked away. I told Chiefy in case there was any comeback, and he told me that Lord Tedder's own

Engineering Officer had told him of this incident. I was expecting to be told off, but I was not, and we soon forgot all about it.

Sometime later, I was called to the Engineering Office, where I was surprised to see Chiefy. I was told that I was being sent on the Instrument Repair Class 1 course at Melksham, and was asked for my reaction to this news. I replied that I was very grateful to be sent on this course, but this was tempered with the fact that I was the least experienced instrument repairer in the workshop, and the others would wonder why they had been passed over. Afterwards, Chiefy told me he had been against my selection, and he was certain that my nomination had come from Lord Tedder's Engineering Officer. I wonder?

Back at Melksham, I restarted the Reading coach and Nelson asked me to take over the Bristol speedway trip on Thursday night. The course passed quickly, and again I passed with credit. I was delighted when I heard that I was being posted to Lasham, near Alton, because this was on a direct line to Woking and only took 30 minutes each way. Jean was also delighted, so we got engaged straight away.

We went up to London specially to buy the engagement ring in Bravington's, which was near the Angel. Jean chose it, and it cost the vast sum of £19. Both of our parents were happy with our decision because we had to have their permission to get married, as we were both under 21. My mum was more keen than Jean's mum - something that lasted until Stephen was born in 1951.

My job at Lasham was a very cushy one. I was one member of a four-man team. Our leader was Sergeant

Bill Cutler, Air Frames; Bill Freeman, Engineer; Ted Bowers, Jack of all trades and driver of one 30 CWT Bedford van, and I was Instruments and Electrics.

Whenever an aircraft crashed in the whole of Southern England, we were one of four teams who would attend and our Sergeant would assess whether the crashed plane was a write-off, or if it could be repaired. If decided a write-off, we would remove all guns, instruments, engines and oxygen equipment for reuse. A Queen Mary low loader trailer would come down from Lasham with the wrecking crew, and we joined forces with them in order to take the wings and under-carriage off and load the frame onto a tractor before taking it to the dump.

Most of our repair work took place in the aircraft's home aerodrome, but the local staff did not have the skills to deal with the required repairs. When we were on these bases we worked in the aircraft workshops where we were our own bosses, doing various difficult repairs.

I got home most weekends, but even so Jean wrote to me every day. The girls in Jean's office used to scribble many messages on the back of the envelope and the letter. They wrote anagrams such as ITALY - 'I trust and love you.' HOLLAND - 'Hope our love lasts and never dies.' And finally, 'Dear postman. Can't you find a nest to which our lovebirds can fly?'

I don't know if the postman was responsible, but one weekend Jean told me that Mr Bayliss, a local landlord, had two rooms for rent available. We decided to get married on the 10th of April 1948. Jean made all the arrangements with the help of the two mums for the wedding. We decided to have a honeymoon at the Prince's Hotel, Torquay - again Jean arranged this too.

Shortly before the wedding, Jean went down to the new home to measure for some new curtains, only to be told by Mrs Bayliss that her husband had let the rooms to an army officer and his wife for twice the rent that we would have paid. This would mean that in the immediate future we would live with Jean's Mum and Dad, whilst Jean looked for accommodation for us to rent.

Saturday 10th April 1948 was a fine, sunny day; an ideal day for a wedding. Jean looked radiant in her wedding dress, and I brought a new, dark blue suit. We got married in Jean's local church at St. Johns. The Vicar kept repeating that we were 'young, very young'. But with the war, it was a very common practice to marry young.

After a splendid wedding breakfast in Trinity Church in Knaphill, we caught the train to Exeter because we could not get down to Torquay that day. Our first night as a married couple was spent in the Imperial Hotel, Exeter, which was next to the station. The next morning, not too early, we made our way to Torquay where we stayed at the Prince's Hotel. This hotel was situated high up above the Imperial Hotel, Torquay, which is where Poirot's stayed in Agatha Christie's 'Peril at End House'. Both Hotels have wonderful sea views.

We were having a nice time, when on the Tuesday morning we came down for breakfast to find a large notice in Reception saying 'Would LAC[5] Ben Flude, please contact reception urgently." Jean and I immediately thought that someone had had an accident. But it was my CO (Commanding Officer) telling me that my leave was cancelled because the whole unit was moving out and going to Lineham in Wiltshire.

I was horrified. So I contacted the CO's office and he rang me back. I reminded him that he had given me leave to get married, and I was in Torquay on my honeymoon and wasn't due to return to Lasham until 8am on Monday 19th of April. There was an agonized wait before he finally said that he would see what he could do for us, and would ring me back as soon as he could.

When he rang, he asked me to report to Lasham on Monday morning, where I would have to help in the final clean-up at Lasham. Jean and I enjoyed the rest of our honeymoon. After getting my usual train, I arrived at Lasham at 8am sharp on the next Monday morning and was greeted by the CO, complete with his chauffeur.

My first job was to go around all the huts and clean everything left behind, including all my bits and pieces which were still in my locker. We helped clean out the offices and huts, and moved the station bikes into the main hangar. I was then given a travel warrant to Cardiff not Lineham, and told that I was to be posted in St. Athans. As I was due to be demobbed in three-months-time, they thought I was needed more at St Athans than at Lineham.

When I arrived at St Athans no one had been informed of my coming, and I found that I was not needed in the instrument shop. However, as they were short staffed in the photographic section, I was enlisted to help with the aerial mapping. The Air Ministry was taking aerial photographs of all RAF airfields because many of them were due to be sold off and some of them extended. It was like doing a giant jigsaw puzzle, fitting all the photographs of the airfields together. There followed a series of odd jobs until my demob in August 1948.

Just before my demob, I had a couple of bad bouts of bronchitis. One while I was playing football and the other while walking with Jean at Newlands Corner. On this latter occasion, my doctor suspected that it was not bronchitis but possibly bronchial asthma.

Jean had found a flat in Littlewick Road, Horsell comprising a large sitting room, dining come bedroom, tiny kitchen and bathroom WC. We were very happy there. I bought Jean a lovely Labrador puppy, which she named Sandy. Jean had dogs all her life. The lady in the upstairs flat looked after Sandy while we were at work. Sadly, he was run over by my doctor's car in our drive and Jean was so upset.

When the winter came, my health got much worse and my doctor sent me to St. Luke's Hospital, where the specialist was Doctor MacMillan. With him, I took the Wasserman tests, which indicated that I was allergic to feathers, grass cuttings and possibly cats. He also thought that I was suffering from sinusitis, and he drained my sinuses - a particularly painful procedure!

Jean and our parents were worried about my health. They thought it was the damp, marshy area at Littlewick Road, so we gave up our flat and moved back in with Jean's mum and dad. Dr *Me on my motorbike with Sandy*

McMillan gave me some tablets to help me with my asthma, which were Franol as a preventative and Ventoline, which was placed under the tongue and gave instant relief from an attack.

In the spring of 1949, Jean, who had kept in touch with Mrs Knight (the landlady of the house in Horsell), was asked if we were interested in having the upstairs of 25 Lakeside Road, Hermitage Estate. They had rented the entire house and the only snag was that we had to share the bathroom, which was on our floor. Of course, we said yes.

It was a great move, and we were very happy there. My health continued to improve and Jean was very content in the new house. Our thoughts turned to the future, as Jean did not want to have a family until she was 21. That would be June 1950 at the earliest.

I was worrying about my future in the drawing office. When I left in 1945, I was number two in the office, when I came back from the RAF I'd been relegated to number seven. Ernie Goater, John Moffat and Eric Hunter had all come back to the office while I was away in the RAF. Where did my future lie?

Printed in Great Britain
by Amazon

51691168R00047